# Garfield

# RIDDLES

By Mark Acey and Scott Nickel

Garfield created by JIM DAVIS

LERNER PUBLICATIONS ◆ MINNEAPOLIS

**Which side of Garfield has the most fur?**
The outside!

Lerner Publications Company
An imprint of Lerner Publishing Group, Inc.
241 First Avenue North
Minneapolis, MN 55401 USA

For reading levels and more information, look up this title at www.lernerbooks.com.

Main body text set in Mikado a Bold. Typeface provided by HVD fonts.

Image credit: Jobalou/DigitalVision Vectors/Getty Images, p. 4.

**Editor:** Allison Juda **Designer:** Susan Rouleau-Fienhage

**Library of Congress Cataloging-in-Publication Data**

Names: Nickel, Scott, author. | Acey, Mark, author.
Title: Garfield's ® riddles / by Mark Acey and Scott Nickel.
Description: Minneapolis : Lerner Publications, [2021] | Series: Garfield's® belly laughs | Audience: Ages: 7-11 | Audience: Grades: 2-3 | Summary: "What's the perfect addition to any jokes book collection? Riddles from Garfield! Stump your friends and laugh out loud with riddles for all occasions that are sure to make even the grumpiest cat bust a gut"— Provided by publisher.
Identifiers: LCCN 2019036662 (print) | LCCN 2019036663 (ebook) | ISBN 9781541589834 (library binding) | ISBN 9781728400259 (ebook)
Subjects: LCSH: Garfield (Fictitious character)—Juvenile literature. | Riddles, Juvenile.
Classification: LCC PN6371.5 N53 2021 (print) | LCC PN6371.5 (ebook) | DDC 818/.602— dc23

LC record available at https://lccn.loc.gov/2019036662
LC ebook record available at https://lccn.loc.gov/2019036663

Manufactured in the United States of America
1-47493-48037-1/14/2020

**What's
Garfield's
favorite way
to sleep?**
Late.

**What follows
Garfield wherever
he goes?**
His tail.

## What has teeth but can't bite?
A comb.

## What is full of holes but holds water?
A sponge.

**What gets wet as it dries?**
A towel.

**What has two legs but can't walk?**
A pair of pants.

IT'S ALL FUN AND GAMES UNTIL YOUR PANTS DON'T FIT ANYMORE

**What always eats but is never full?**
Garfield.

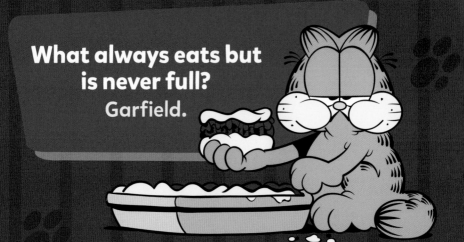

**What can Garfield take but not give back?**
A nap.

**What is Garfield's favorite mountain?**
Mt. Ever-rest!

**What would you get if you crossed a flying boy with a bear?**
Peter Panda!

**Who's orange and furry and doesn't like Toto?**
The Wizard of Paws.

TOTO WOULD BE BETTER IF HE WERE A CAT

**What would you get if you crossed a cartoon dog with a cow?**
Scooby-Moo!

**What would you get if you crossed Garfield with Quasimodo?**
The Munchcat of Notre Dame.

**What would you get if you crossed Dracula with Odie?**

A vampire who slobbers on your neck!

CATS RULE

DOGS DROOL

**How can you tell when you have a slow dog?**

He brings you yesterday's newspaper.

**What does Odie do when it rains?**
He gets wet!

**Why did Garfield wear sneakers?**
So he could sneak up on Odie!

WILL I SHARE MY UMBRELLA? I'LL LET YOU GUESS

11

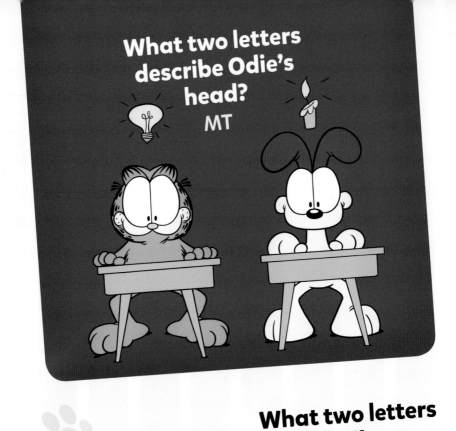

What two letters describe Odie's head?
MT

What two letters describe a slippery street?
IC

What two letters does Garfield most like to watch?
TV

**What's just as big as Garfield but doesn't weigh a single pound?**
Garfield's shadow!

**Why did Garfield take a ruler to bed?**
To see how long he slept.

**Why did Garfield take a bath after stealing Odie's dinner?**
He wanted to make a clean getaway.

**Is Garfield afraid of man-eating sharks?**
No, he's afraid of cat-eating sharks.

I WANT TO BE THE ONE WHO DOES THE EATING

**What did the little cob call its father?**
Pop corn!

**What has feathers, webbed feet, and rows of razor-sharp teeth?**
A Great White Duck.

**Where do vampires keep their money?**
In a blood bank.

**What keys don't open doors?**
Donkeys, monkeys, and turkeys.

THE KEY TO MY HEART IS FOOD

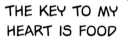

**What kind of bath can you take without water?**

A sun bath.

**What has four legs and flies?**

A picnic table.

**What kind of dog should you wear on your head in winter?**
Earmutts.

**Why do hummingbirds hum?**
They forgot the words!

**Where did Odie sleep when he went camping?**
In a pup tent!

**What's the difference between a dog and a flea?**
A dog can have fleas, but a flea can't have dogs!

DOGS . . . YOU CAN'T LIVE WITH 'EM AND YOU CAN'T LIVE WITHOUT 'EM

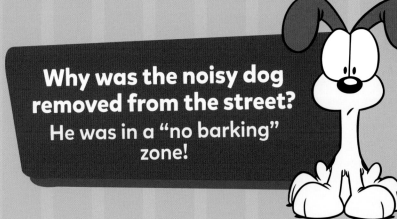

**Why was the noisy dog removed from the street?**
He was in a "no barking" zone!

**What do you give a dog with a fever?**
Mustard. It's the best thing for a hot dog!

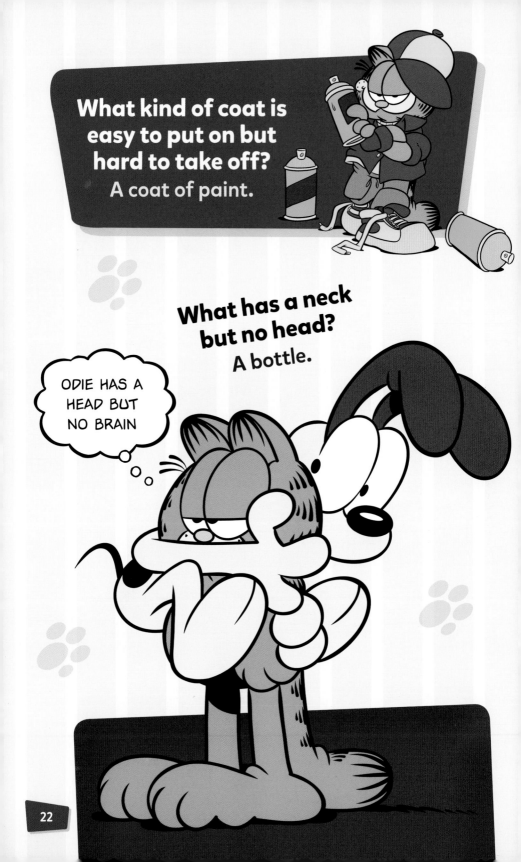

**What kind of coat is easy to put on but hard to take off?**
A coat of paint.

**What has a neck but no head?**
A bottle.

ODIE HAS A HEAD BUT NO BRAIN

What kind of music
do mummies like?
Wrap music!

What would you get if you
crossed an automobile
with a water park?
A carpool!

**What do you call a pirate who always skips school?**
Captain Hooky!

**What did the space alien get for his school report?**
Extraterrestrial credit!

IF LIFE IS A TEST, I WANT A CHEAT SHEET!

**Where do genies go on summer vacation?**
To lamp camp!

**What do you call a kitten that does somersaults in the air?**
An acrocat.

Where was the Declaration of Independence signed?
On the bottom.

What's the best way to keep a bull from charging?
Take away his credit cards!

**Why does Garfield spend so much time sleeping?**
Because he can.

Z

**What would you get if you crossed Garfield with a canary?**
One less canary.

**Why did Garfield throw Nermal into the snow?**
He wanted Nermal to chill out!

**Why did Garfield put insect spray on Jon's watch?**
Because it was full of ticks.

THANKS A LOT, GARFIELD

**What's the hardest thing about playing water polo?**
Finding a horse that can swim!

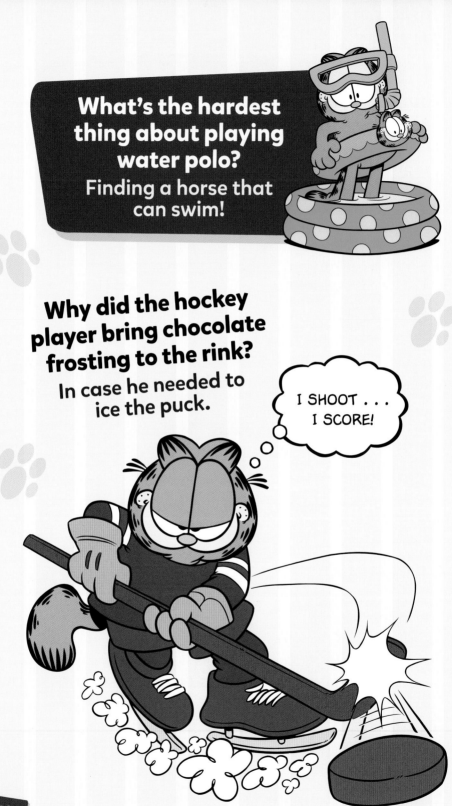

**Why did the hockey player bring chocolate frosting to the rink?**
In case he needed to ice the puck.

I SHOOT . . . I SCORE!

# Why did the hurried bowler want to roll a strike?

## Because he had no time to spare.

# Why did the surfer cross the ocean?

## To get to the other tide.

**What do you call Odie after Garfield sprays him with water?**
A soggy doggy!

**How is Garfield like a flower?**
He's usually found in a bed.

SWEET DREAMS